MW00583174

Made New: New Believers Devotional
Author Dr. Dave C Joseph Jr.
Devoted.love

Designer Phill Stroh
stroh.design

Editors
Sarah Madden
Linda Joseph

Made New: New Believers Devotional
Copyright © 2021 by Dave C. Joseph Jr.
Published by Sheep Dog Publications
Trade paperback ISBN: 978-1-944634-06-3
ePub ISBN: 978-1-944634-03-2
Mobipocket ISBN: 978-1-944634-04-9.

Presented To:

_____

By:

_____

On:

_____

Mobilizing Moments

Devoted.Love

Dear Child of God,

Welcome and congratulations! You are a part of the Family of God. Heaven is celebrating because you made a decision on _____/_____/_____ to be a follower of Jesus. Budget time in your schedule daily to be with God. You are what the world needs because you have the light of Christ, so do not be afraid to be transparent about what God is doing and has done in your life.

My hope and prayer for you, Chosen one, is that as you journey with Christ these scriptures, names of God and so much more will encourage you to do more than you think is possible because you are a Child of God. Embrace the Words of God, memorize them, share them, and listen to the Spirit of God.

This book is a sacrifice to God to help you Abide in Christ by encouraging you to live out the love you have been shown in ways that encourage you to be more like Christ. If we do not meet on earth, I look forward to meeting you in the presence of Jesus.

May the love of God keep your heart solely centered in the truth of what Christ has done for you. Know that the Spirit of God is communicating with God on your behalf. May the peace of God rest upon you as you celebrate that God has created you for this time and has no desire to ruin you, just to grow you. May God bless you with a spiritual mentor. May the joy of God keep you smiling in the midst of any storm because your eyes are locked onto the One True God, the God of Grace.

I thank God for you!

Your Brother in Christ,

Dave C. Joseph Jr.
Devoted.Love

Growth Guide

This book was created to support you on your journey with Christ as you grow deeper roots by embracing seasons filled with a new family that comes with its own values and culture. Welcome to a family that runs throughout history and is all over the world. If people around you believe in Christ, it is important for you to find a person or people who can journey with you spiritually as you follow Christ.

Many times, the person who pointed you to Christ will be the person to help you get started on your journey. What matters the most is that you find someone who has surrendered their life to Christ as their Lord and Savior, is dedicated to reading the Bible and is in a healthy relationship with God, praying, listening, and obeying God daily. Check that they are doing this and then ask them if they are willing to meet at least weekly to discuss what God is doing in both of your lives. (They don't need to be much older than you spiritually to walk with you because this journey is spiritual. The tandem version of this book is to help them walk with you.)

As you stay close to God, you will feel the love of God and be filled with a joy that is not based on what is happening but on who you are in Him. Part of God's love will be seen through times of pruning, correction, and seasons filled with bearing eternal fruit, as in Galatians 5:22. Take each day to work with God as He transforms you from the inside out and as He transforms the world around you through you and through other children of God.

This devotional is designed to help you understand more of who you are in Christ. Make the most of every moment by taking your time to read the words of God and by ruminating (mentally continue chewing) on it throughout the mornings, days, or weeks. This devotional is not meant to be rushed through or even done in order. It was written to encourage you

This book was created to support you on your journey with Christ as you grow deeper roots by embracing seasons filled with a new family that comes with its own values and culture. Welcome to a family that runs throughout history and is all over the world. If people around you believe in Christ, it is important for you to find a person or people who can journey with you spiritually as you follow Christ.

Many times, the person who pointed you to Christ will be the person to help you get started on your journey. What matters the most is that you find someone who has surrendered their life to Christ as their Lord and Savior, is dedicated to reading the Bible and is in a healthy relationship with God, praying, listening, and obeying God daily. Check that they are doing this and then ask them if they are willing to meet at least weekly to discuss what God is doing in both of your lives. (They don't need to be much older than you spiritually to walk with you because this journey is spiritual. The tandem version of this book is to help them walk with you.)

As you stay close to God, you will feel the love of God and be filled with a joy that is not based on what is happening but on who you are in Him. Part of God's love will be seen through times of pruning, correction, and seasons filled with bearing eternal fruit, as in Galatians 5:22. Take each day to work with God as He transforms you from the inside out and as He transforms the world around you through you and through other children of God.

This devotional is designed to help you understand more of who you are in Christ. Make the most of every moment by taking your time to read the words of God and by ruminating (mentally continue chewing) on it throughout the mornings, days, or weeks. This devotional is not meant to be rushed through or even done in order. It was written to encourage you to go deeper and take your time in building a relationship. Relationship cannot be rushed but it can be neglected if we approach it with a goal of consuming the information for personal gain. This devotional is designed to keep your heart and head connected to the will of God as you worship Him daily.

The first page of each moment has scriptures that are great for memorizing but more importantly they are better for living out. One chapter of the Bible is assigned to each moment, and all twelve books of the Made New series will lead you through most of the Bible. The name of God describes the relationship a sibling in Christ had with God in the past that you can use as a steppingstone to grow your relationship with Him. In each moment I have tried to write to you as if we were meeting daily for 15 minutes to spur you on to do the good work of obeying God. My words are based on scripture but are not scripture. Examine everything and everyone against the Bible! The last part of every moment is extra credit. It is a word of the moment found in one of the native languages of the Bible followed by scriptures that use that word in context.

The second page of each moment has two parts:
1. Know, Grow, Go and **2. Flow, Sow and Get Low.**

Know – What did you learn in reading the Bible?

Grow – What can you apply to yourself and do?

Go – What are you feeling challenged to live out today?

Flow – How did you work with God in light of what you learned?

Sow – I shared my story about Christ with…?

Get Low – Track your conversations with God and your requests and praises. How much is about others?

Throughout the book you will also see four images that

are on the cover of the book, water, plant, wind and fire. Each image is an icon to encourage you to wrestle with your relationship with God. As you are challenged to grow, color the icons that mirror your moment with God.

Water / Identification with Jesus
Embracing His death, burial and resurrection

Plant / Spiritual Growth
Dying to self, stretching to bear eternal fruit

Wind / Holy Spirit
Faithful focus, slowing down to listen to God

Fire / Holiness
Resisting old nature, living purposefully for God

I encourage you to add spiritual disciplines to each moment and use good websites like blueletterbible.org to research and learn more about the Bible. At the end of the book are pages to record people that God has put on your heart to pray for to join the family. You have been made new in Christ and there is much to learn about our infinite God. Daily Enjoy.

Good News ROMANS 6:22-23

Moment 1 – Luke 1
Savor & Reflect: Romans 3:23–24
    God: Elohim (God, Creator and Faithful One)
    Genesis 1:1–10
Ruminating Prayer: Thank you for the Gift of Eternal Life through Jesus Christ.

Welcome, fully experience your new relationship with your God, the God of Creation. He chose you before you were born to be loved and to know love in Him. God has plans for your life that require all of you. Your body, mind, and spirit now belong to God because you chose Jesus as your Lord. Daily fears are left at the Cross because neither death nor any other thing defines you. Big or small take it to God.

In your journey with Jesus, every day you are challenged not to look at things as the world does but to engage with God—our Heavenly Father, Jesus, and the Holy Spirit—in the center of your thoughts and actions. His plan for your life includes being part of the family of God, in Christ. Like Mary with the words she would share about the good news, you have good news to share about what has happened in your life.

Hebrew: לִגְאַל (gâ'al) – redeemer, avenger, restorer
Romans 3:23, 6:23, 5:8, 10:9–10, 10:13, Genesis 1:1–2, James 4:12

Thank you:

Know: (Personalize a Bible verse from the day by rewriting it as a prayer to God.)
I know...

Grow: I believe...
I am...

Go: I will...

Flow: Where did I see God working today?
I partnered with Him by?

Sow: I shared my faith today by?

Get Low – Prayer Request: Please Jesus, I need...
Take 3 minutes to be quiet before God to listen in prayer.

Child of God 1 JOHN 3:1-10

Moment 2 – Luke 2
Savor & Reflect: John 1:12
    God: Elohim (God, Creator and Faithful One)
    Genesis 1:11-21
Ruminating Prayer: I am God's child. Thank You!

Welcome to a new day as a new creation. You are a new creation in God! As you start and end this day, do not lose sight of the change that God has done in your life. By professing with your mouth and believing in your heart that Jesus the Christ paid for your sins through His death, burial, and resurrection, you joined the family of God. Family members know God through His actions, His words, and His Spirit. His words and actions are in the Bible, and His Spirit is in you.

The more you get into the Bible, the more you will understand who you are, your relationship with God, and His expectations for you. As a member of God's family, culture, structure, language, love, and identity are just a few of the things that change. As a child of God, make this day a day to share with others that you were removed from an old state of a sinner and are in a new state, saint. Thank God as you celebrate your second birthday, the day that you accepted God's gift as payment for all your sins, past, present, and future. The birthday of your spiritual awakening and union with God is a day that you should strive to remember—add it to your calendar.

Hebrew: הָעוּשִׁי (yĕshuw`ah) – salvation, deliverance, victory

Genesis 1:27, Galatians 3:26, 1 John 3:1–2,10, Galatians 4:6–8

Thank you:

Know:

Grow:

Go:

14

Flow:

Sow:

Get Low:

Debt Free EPHESIANS 2:5-6

Moment 3 – Luke 3
Savor & Reflect: Romans 6:1–6
    God: Elohim (God, Creator and Faithful One)
    Genesis 1:22–31
Ruminating Prayer: I dedicate my life to You; lead me today. You are my Lord!

You have been delivered from a debt that you could not pay. Just as important is that you are now free to love, talk to, and hear from your God the Creator, the designer of relationship. God created you for a loving relationship with Him and others, but it is only in Him that you can really understand true sacrificial love. Love by the world's standard is all about self. Love by God's standard is all about others. He wants you to love others like He loves you, sacrificially, fully, humbly and sincerely.

You are free today to not walk in sin. Sin no longer rules you. You are no longer a disciple of the world, Satan. You are free to engage God about everything through prayer, the Bible, and Christ centered spiritual leaders who encourage you in your journey with Christ. Make more time to read the Bible, God's words, to discover who you are and to whom you belong.

Greek: συσταυρόω (systauróō) – crucified with

Colossians 1:13–14, Genesis 2:4, Mark 15:32, Romans 6:6

Thank you:

Know:

Grow:

Go:

Flow:

Sow:

Get Low:

Hope EPHESIANS 2:5-6

Moment 4 – Luke 4
Savor & Reflect: Colossians 1:27
    God: Adonai (Master, My Lord)
    Genesis 15:2, 8, 18:3
Ruminating Prayer: Jesus, my redeemer, is with me and in me. Amen.

What we place our hope in affects how we see and engage with the world around us. Daily we place our trust in things and systems that we cannot see or understand. This is the definition of living by faith. When we take action based on our faith, we are living in Hope. Our Hope is in Christ! Our hope is in the work of Jesus.

You are created to worship and to do it daily, moment by moment. Worship is keeping God, Jesus, the Father, and the Holy Spirit in the front of your thinking. Worship the Lord your God with a hope that is not like those who do not believe in Christ or have a relationship with Him. Your hope is based on what Jesus did on the cross for you and for every other person on earth.

You were created to serve. What you serve is what you worship. How you spend time and money and how you engage with relationships tells what you worship. Whom will you serve today? Choose to worship Christ!

Greek: ἐλπίς (el-pe's) – to anticipate, normally with pleasure, expectation, confidence

Psalm 147:11, Jeremiah 29:11,
1 Corinthians 13:13, 2 Corinthians 5:11

Thank you:

Know:

Grow:

Go:

Flow:

Sow:

Get Low:

23

New Creation 2 CORINTHIANS 5:17

Moment 5 – Luke 5
Savor & Reflect: Galatians 6:15
    God: Adonai (Master, My Lord)
    Genesis 18:27, 30, 31, 32
Ruminating Prayer: I am a new creation in Christ,
my past does not define me.

You are a new creation in Him, and you are created with a purpose that can only be found in journeying with Him. The journey is not for the weak of will but for those who are willing to put God first, others second, and self third. This means your dreams, ideas, and actions should be based and brought before Christ daily as you pray and as you study His Word, the Bible. You are no longer a sinner but a saint. Yet daily you must recognize that you live in a fallen world and still have the ability to sin. Renew your mind with God's word daily so your movements will become milestones in your faith filled journey with Christ.

Will you launch out into the deep with Christ? Will you let Him bless you in ways that boggle your mind? Will you embrace the blessings or the blesser? Often, we look for God to solve our problems in ways that make sense when in reality we are called to follow Christ, not lead Him.

Greek: νέος (ne'-os) – recently born, young, new

Ephesians 4:24, Colossians 3:10, 1 Corinthians 5:7, Colossians 3:10

Thank you:

Know:

Grow:

Go:

Flow:

Sow:

Get Low:

Love and Obey DEUTERONOMY 11:1

Moment 6 – Luke 6
Savor & Reflect: Deuteronomy 10:12
    God: Adonai (Master, My Lord)
    Genesis 20:4, Exodus 4:13, 5:22
Ruminating Prayer: My Lord, grow my love for Your commands.

From the group who followed Christ, Jesus chose those who would be close to him. He challenged His followers to understand in word and deed the heavy requirements of being a disciple of Christ. He did not promise followers blessings unless they were willing to be cursed for Him. He did not tell them about what they would get but told them to give and give more because He has given so much.

God's love language is obedience. His love language is not like ours. God's love language is centered in His love, holiness, justice, peace, and patience. His love language is best understood when we recognize He wants what is best for us, even when He corrects us.

We are part of something bigger than we can understand because God—Jesus—asks us to love Him with a different definition than we find in the world. God's definition, our definition in Him, is one where we keep the desires and will of the other before our own desires. The world defines lust as love, because lust puts ourselves first. We are to be known for living out love and mercy because of the grace we have experienced.

Hebrew: בַהַא ('ahab) – human love for another, human desire for things, human love for God.

Genesis 22:2, 29:18, 37:4, Leviticus 19:18

Thank you:

Know:

Grow:

Go:

30

Flow:

Sow:

Get Low:

Reflection LUKE 7

What does Salvation mean to you?

Moment 7 – Let Christ be your standard, ask for help with weakness, and celebrate His work in your life.

What have you learned through the last seven moments in your relationship with God?

What will you do today that is different because of what you learned?

What step will you do to make this a habit?

What was your favorite Bible verse(s) from the last few moments and why?

What was your favorite name for God so far and why?

Adoption MARK 3:31-35

Moment 8 – Luke 8
Savor & Reflect: Romans 8:27
    God: Jehovah Jireh (The Lord will provide, God of
    Fellowship, Self-Existent) Genesis 22:14
Ruminating Prayer: I am your child, God. Your Spirit is
within me. Lead me, please!

This is the day the Lord has made, and it is not promised
that it will go as planned, especially if we follow Jesus.
The woman who was healed by and through her faith in
Jesus had to leave her past to step into a new present.
She had to let go of her old identity to face the world in
the freedom that could only be explained as she lived
out her faith.

She chose to go to Jesus for help, and we must do that
and so much more. She chose to go to Him because of
the change that He made in the life of others around and
with Him. As you journey with Him today, share the love,
joy, and hope that He has given you with those who are
hurting around you. Open your eyes in Christ!

Family can be amazing when you feel loved and known. In our family we are loved and known, and so much more. In this family, every person has roles and responsibilities in their relationships with others. Our Father is our love and leader. He controls our day, which means we must yield control of every moment in it, including our burdens and blessings.

Greek: ἅγιος (hä'-ge-os) – most holy thing, a saint

Matthew 12:46–50, Luke 8:19–21, Ephesians 1:9, 1 John 2:17

Thank you:

Know:

Grow:

Go:

Flow:

Sow:

Get Low:

Adoption PSALM 68:5-6

Moment 9 – Luke 9
Savor & Reflect: 1 Peter 5:6–7
   God: Jehovah Jireh (The Lord will provide, God of
   Fellowship, Self-Existent) Genesis 22:14
Ruminating Prayer: Help me to live for what You care
about.

We have been adopted into a spiritual family that crosses race, gender, education, and income. We are joint heirs with Christ. He is our spiritual brother, our redeemer and savior. We are family with God. Jesus is unique and is part of a triune relationship with the other equal parts of God, living in perfect love and harmony.

Who is Jesus to you? Others mention Jesus' name in ways that put Him down or lift Him up, but who is He to you? The disciples experienced Jesus as more than one thing. They saw their Savior was not simply defined by dying for their sins, because He had a personal relationship with them that was more than that from a king, president, or other powerful person. The Bible differentiates between man and Jesus, our Heavenly Father, and the Living Spirit of God.

Jesus came to be known and to know mankind personally. Jesus wants to know you, and for you to know Him. He is infinite and asks you to follow Him. Peter called Him Master and Lord, walked with Him on water, watched as He commanded nature and fed five thousand men with a kid's meal. Peter failed in faith, BUT by following God daily, he grew THROUGH the process of forgiveness by staying close to God.

Hebrew: הָחִיחָצ (tsekh·e·khä') – parched or scorched land, scorched.

Deuteronomy 11:4, 32:3, Hosea 6:3, Psalm 51:10, Matthew 6:28–29

Thank you:

Know:

Grow:

Go:

Flow:

Sow:

Get Low:

Adoption MATTHEW 18:2-4

Moment 10 – Luke 10
Savor & Reflect: Luke 10:37
    God: Jehovah Jireh (The Lord will provide, God of
    Fellowship, Self-Existent) Genesis 22:14
Ruminating Prayer: I yield myself today to loving my
neighbor.

If you could tell your five-year-old self something, what
would it be and why?

Children do not carry the pressures of the world
because everything is greater than they are. Children
ask questions continually because truth must be heard,
learned, and applied. They are constant learners.
Children live out humility by not thinking highly of
themselves and by giving grace and mercy daily because
they are innocent.

Humility is not weakness by God's definition but is the mindset we must internalize as a child of God. Humility does not mean you consider yourself less than someone else. Humility means you understand where your power lies; it resides within your Heavenly Father, Jesus, and the Living Spirit of God. All three are with you today. Take a step closer by humbling yourself like a child and ask, "How can I be more childlike today in my relationship with God?"

Hebrew: תְּמוּד (dem·üth') – likeness, in the likeness of, similitude

Genesis 5:1–3, 2 Kings 16:10, Ezekiel 1:5, Daniel 10:16

Thank you:

Know:

Grow:

Go:

Flow:

Sow:

Get Low:

45

Communion JOHN 14:16-17

Moment 11 – Luke 11
Savor & Reflect: 2 Thessalonians 2:13
    God: Jehovah-Raah (The Lord My Shepherd)
    Genesis 48:15, 49:24, Psalm 23:1, 80:1
Ruminating Prayer: Thank You, God, for choosing me to be a part of Your family and giving me a part of You.

Prayer is a conversation between you and God. It can be a conversation with God, your heavenly Father, Jesus, or the Holy Spirit who lives within you. The Comforter, The Holy Spirit is with you now and always. Jesus is interceding for you because you have accepted His payment for your sins and for Him to be the Lord of your life. Your Heavenly Father loved you so much that He sent His Son to die for you.

Communion with God begins with a decision to accept the work that Christ does for you, daily. Your decision to follow Christ cannot be undone, but it must be practiced daily because you are in a relationship with Him. Prayer can be a word, a sentence, or a walk through the park talking to God with your headphones on. With any conversation, listening is important. Make time daily to listen to God by being still for part of your time of prayer, by reading the Bible, and by listening to siblings who are further in their journey with Christ.

Hebrew: רָחָב (bä·khar') – to choose, chosen, elect

Exodus 17:9, 18:25, Deuteronomy 7:7, 10:15, 12:11

Thank you:

Know:

Grow:

Go:

Flow:

Sow:

Get Low:

Adoption EPHESIANS 6:17-18

Moment 12 – Luke 12
Savor & Reflect: Romans 6:4
    God: Jehovah-Raah (The Lord My Shepherd)
    Genesis 48:15, 49:24, Psalm 23:1, 80:1
Ruminating Prayer: Let my life in You blind me to the distractions that lead to death in the world.

In your relationship with God and His people, your family, you no longer must wear a mask or pretend to be perfect. Believers are not perfect. We are sinners who have been made perfect in the eyes of God because of Jesus' death and resurrection. When you accepted Christ and His work, He accepted you in your brokenness to work with and worship Him.

Pharisees, in the Bible, lived their lives with a focus on God's law. They lived and elevated themselves by adding rules to the law to "protect" people from their sinful nature. These sinners in robes saw themselves as better than others because they felt they could pay for their sin through works.

There is no work you can or will do that can save you. Anything you do outside of the will of God and before the leading of His Spirit is for self and leads nowhere. Today, do everything for God, and let Him take care of everything. Fear is often the basis for our decisions but now we live in faith. You are filled and overflowing with love and grace! U R Family!

Greek: πλεονεξία (ple-o-ne-kse'-ä) – covetousness, greediness, avarice

Ephesians 4:19, 5:3, Colossians 3:5, 2 Peter 2:3

Thank you:

Know:

Grow:

Go:

Flow:

Sow:

Get Low:

Adoption EPHESIANS 3:14-21

Moment 13 – Luke 13
Savor & Reflect: Psalm 62:8
    God: Jehovah-Raah (The Lord My Shepherd)
    Genesis 48:15, 49:24, Psalm 23:1, 80:1
Ruminating Prayer: I will wait until You say go… because You are my true love.

Fake plants are great for making a room look beautiful. Fake trees are great for providing shade. Fake fruit? It looks good but is not good to eat. As a child of God, you are called to produce spiritual fruit by growing in spiritual maturity and journeying with others to encourage them to accept Christ.

Do not just show outward signs of belief. Allow Him to bear spiritual fruit in your life. You are created for a deeper purpose, because you have a new home, heaven. You are a citizen of the Kingdom of God, the Kingdom of Heaven, and investing in it requires you to obey, to love.

You cannot lose your relationship with God. You can allow other things in your life to crowd Him out. Your life is lost to Him as an unfair gift because Jesus is perfect and you are a broken vessel. He deemed you worthy of His love. Jesus gave His life for you, and now you belong to Him. To belong and be part of something bigger than yourself and your understanding is family. You are a part of a family that exists outside of time because you have eternal life. Jesus' gift of life will not be fully understood until you stand in His presence. You are free from your sin. You are free in Him! Celebrate and share this truth.

Greek: ἀγωνίζομαι (ä-go-ne'-zo-mi) – contend with struggles, fight, to endeavor with strenuous zeal

John 18:36, 1 Corinthians 9:25, Colossians 1:29, 4:12

Thank you:

Know:

Grow:

Go:

Flow:

Sow:

Get Low:

Lord's Supper 1 CORINTHIANS 11:23-26

Moment 14 – Luke 14
Savor & Reflect: 1 Peter 3:18
    God: Yahweh (Lord, Master, Jehovah)
    Genesis 2:4-9,15-22
Ruminating Prayer: I am only saved because of Your righteousness.

Eating food with each other and spending time together is part of being family in Christ. Relationship is built and depth is found by experiencing the freedom of love, being known, and communing at the dinner table of Grace and Truth.

You are invited to a banquet, a banquet hosted by God where no expense has been spared. This invitation does require you to leave the place where you are and go to a different place. He requires you to leave what you know for what He has prepared. There is a cost, a cross you must individually carry with Christ to experience the fullness of this banquet and fellowship. Joy is found in letting Jesus work in and through you by co-laboring to make Him known to all.

To bear your cross means you give your burdens to Jesus daily and you yield your plans before His, throughout the day. To bear your cross means to forgive in the same way you have been forgiven, freely. To bear your cross means you rest in the work of Jesus and share the invitation of fellowship with those who are not like you, individuals looking for bread, and needing the Bread of Life.

Hebrew: הָנָע (ä·nä') – to afflict, to humble, to be made low

Genesis 16:6 & 9, Exodus 10:3, 22:22–23, Leviticus 16:29 & 31

Thank you:

Know:

Grow:

Go:

Flow:

Sow:

Get Low:

But God ROMANS 5:12-15

Moment 15 – Luke 15
Savor & Reflect: Psalm 49:14-15
    God: Yahweh (Lord, Master, Jehovah)
    Genesis 24
Ruminating Prayer: You redeemed me and gave me a unique purpose.

All of heaven rejoiced when you chose to follow Jesus. God with His angels rejoiced when you accepted your new name and value, more precious than gold. He sought you out even when you did not yet love Him. He sacrificed for you because He deemed you worth it. He has made you Holy for His purpose and worship. God loves you!

His love for you is the same love He wants every person to experience. Your purpose is not to be filled with the things of the world but with love for Him and others. Your purpose is not your job, house, or income. Your purpose in life is to overflow with the Spirit of God, to share the truth of your transformation from death to life in Jesus. His plan for your life is for you to worship and glorify God with all of your heart, in every area of your life, every day into and throughout eternity.

Let us live out our purpose by worshiping God with our entire body and spirit!

Greek: ἀναζάω (ä-nä-zä'-o) – to live again, to be restored, to revive

Luke 15:32, Romans 7:9, 14:9

Thank you:

Know:

Grow:

Go:

Flow:

Sow:

Get Low:

But God ROMANS 8:33-39

Moment 16 – Luke 16
Savor & Reflect: Matthew 19:26
    God: Yahweh (Lord, Master, Jehovah)
    Deuteronomy 4
Ruminating Prayer: I yield to You. With You, all things are possible!

Nothing can separate you from the love of God. The Father, Son, and Holy Spirit are in a full relationship with themselves. And, as they are the origin of love, you are loved sacrificially. God is three unique parts that exist in unity and are the origin of everything, including community. All three parts of God must be embraced to understand the triune way we are to love others.

Triune love requires us to see the physical, spiritual, and relational side to people, places, and things. Because of Christ, your spirit has been made new and now desires to be with, work with, and be filled with God. This affects how you engage with physical things around you including your body. Relationships will change when you bring Christ into every situation. This is how we begin to live out love.

We show God love by being faithful to all three parts of Him, by putting His desires above our own, by using our mind and money to love others sacrificially, and by making intentional moments to obey. When we sacrificially love the less fortunate, when we wrestle with and memorize God's Words and use them to point others to Him through our actions, when we realize that time is short and embrace our new nature over our old, we begin to live out love.

Greek: πιστός (pe-sto's) – faithful, can be relied on, believe, true

Matthew 25:21 & 23, Luke 12:42, 16:10, 19:17

Thank you:

Know:

Grow:

Go:

Flow:

Sow:

Get Low:

But God COLOSSIANS 1:13-16

Moment 17 – Luke 17
Savor & Reflect: Romans 5:8
    God: Jehovah Nissi (The Lord My Banner)
    Exodus 17:15
Ruminating Prayer: Your love for me when I did not love You humbles me. Use me today!

Grace and mercy are often spoken of together in the Bible. Grace is favoring people who do not deserve it in ways that make them better than they could make themselves. Grace is beautiful to experience and gives dignity to the receiver. Mercy is shielding or holding back a person from the fully deserved response for their actions. Mercy and grace are part of God's love toward us, the world.

Jesus gives grace and mercy to those in need. He gives in ways that transform our lives because we are willing to ask for help. Asking for help means we recognize we are not in power, but He is. Our circumstances do not determine our options or opportunities. Our God has everything we need. We must ask continually and clearly for God to align our hearts with His will. We must be humble because we are made of dust, He sustains our life, and He is our God.

God does not need anyone. He wants to use you. He desires for you to do more than say thank you and tell Him what you want. He expects you to love Him by doing more than following rules. He is your loving King! He wants you to serve Him in ways that build on and into the relationship found in Jesus. What can you do today to make God smile?

Hebrew: תאַטָּח (khat·tä·ä') – sin, condition of sin, offering for sin

Genesis 18:20, Exodus 29:14 & 36, 30:10

Thank you:

Know:

Grow:

Go:

Flow:

Sow:

Get Low:

But God COLOSSIANS 2:9-14

Moment 18 – Luke 18
Savor & Reflect: Ephesians 2:1-5
    God: Jehovah Nissi (The Lord My Banner)
    Exodus 17:15
Ruminating Prayer: You are rich in mercy, and Your love is so much more than I deserve.

"But God, I need this money to live!" You can almost hear the rich man saying that as he walked away from God, the creator of the world. This man could not see that his life, breath, mind, house, friends, and every other blessing came from God and that he was being offered something far greater, freedom from sin and the gift of eternal life with the all-powerful God. The Kingdom of God was rejected because the rich man felt the cost was too great to justify having eternal life.

A trick of the Devil that can be seen throughout the entire Bible, from the Garden of Eden to when Judas traded God for silver and is seen in the letters to the Church, is to get the people of God to focus on putting themselves before God. Do not take the bait. Submit every thought, question, and action to our justifying God.

Justification is when God sees you through Christ's sacrifice for your sins. God is the judge and will judge all of creation in light of His plan and His Holiness. He sees you as innocent because the penalty for your sins has been paid. He sees you as a righteous person. Jesus' righteousness was and is applied to you, and in the eyes of God you are in a state of right relationship with Him. As a child of God, revel in the joy of the Lord! Your sins are forgiven.

Greek: δυνατός (dü-nä-to's) – able, powerful, strong

Matthew 26:39, Mark 9:23, 10:27, Acts 2:24

Thank you:

Know:

Grow:

Go:

Flow:

Sow:

Get Low:

But God 1 CORINTHIANS 6:11

Moment 19 – Luke 19
Savor & Reflect: Galatians 1:15–16
    God: Jehovah Nissi (The Lord My Banner)
    Exodus 17:15
Ruminating Prayer: My past is not my present; today my purpose is to follow You.

Cause and effect. For every action there is a reaction. This is presented as a truth in life, but when you know God it becomes clearer that there is no opposite to God. The opposite of love is apathy. Love is infinite because God is infinite. Love does have boundaries and desires for the best to be known because what is found in relationship with God is the best. Nothing on earth is better than the love of God, seen in the fullness of His relationship with mankind. The things that matter the most in life, spiritual things, have more value and make a deeper impact than the things we often give God's time to. We must daily live for spiritual growth over physical gain.

You are uniquely created for this time, space, and place to be used by God for His purpose. When you understand who you are in Him, your position in life becomes less of a factor because He is in charge. He will use you where you are today to impact lives in ways you cannot understand until you stand in His presence. Your body is made of flesh and blood, but that is not who you are. You are a spirit that is housed in flesh and blood. Your spirit, the part of you that you cannot see, is what matters the most to God. Jesus Christ died for all of you. God has granted you this day to be an agent for change. What spiritual thing is God showing you that needs to be changed?

Greek: ἀκολουθέω (ä-ko-lü-the'-o) – to follow the one before you, to join as a disciple

Matthew 8:10, 19, 22–23

Thank you:

Know:

Grow:

Go:

Flow:

Sow:

Get Low:

But God MATTHEW 26:28

Moment 20 – Luke 20
Savor & Reflect: Acts 7:9
    God: Jehovah Tsidkenu (The Lord Our Righteousness)
    Jeremiah 23:6, 33:16
Ruminating Prayer: What others mean for bad, God will use for His glory.

Where do you fit? Do you view information as power? The world encourages us to get money and power so we can control the things around us. Yet the older we get, the more wisdom we glean, the more we realize comfort is not a good goal, because we have much less control over our lives than the world around us would lead us to believe.

Are you an expert in the law, or a follower in faith? God allows those who profess wisdom to miss opportunities because they are not humbled and not seeking to learn about Him. When we focus on learning and walking with God, we end up in a relationship with and within Him. When we focus on the law of death and sin instead of the love and grace found in Christ, we become blinded by self-interest and desires. Daily give God the things that belong to Him! You fit in God's hand, and nothing—and no one—can remove you from Him. You belong to Him.

Greek: ἀποδίδωμι (ä-po-de'-do-me) – to give away with a profit, to pay off, to give back

Matthew 6:6, 18, 12:36, 16:27, 20:8

Thank you:

Know:

Grow:

Go:

Flow:

Sow:

Get Low:

But God ROMANS 4:1-11

Moment 21 – Luke 21
Savor & Reflect: 1 Corinthians 10:13
    God: Jehovah Tsidkenu (The Lord Our Righteousness)
    Jeremiah 23:6, 33:16
Ruminating Prayer: Every time I struggle with temptation, I will run to You and ask for help.

Faith is being sure of what and who you place your hope in and being fully convinced of Jesus, God, when you cannot see Him. In faith, when the widow gave all she had, God noticed. She clearly communicated her love. She lived in a broken world where she could have fed herself or invested in for tomorrow. Instead she put God first, above herself, by giving everything out of faith and communicating to God that she loved Him.

Communications can be classified into at least six levels between God and mankind: transactional conversations that are basic in nature, cooperative exchanges that are friendly verbal interactions, problem-solving discussions that include dealing with relationship issues, discussions that lead to a common language and behavioral interactions, truth sharing that starts in the heart and works through negative and positive feelings, and "I Love You" exchanges that give life, bring clarity, and allow us to dream together. These are types of conversations that we should strive to have with God daily.

Often people give to God out of duty instead of out of relationship. Our relationship with God can be seen in how our actions communicate what is in our hearts. May our words and actions be acceptable in the sight of God as we give Him the offering of this day.

Greek: πᾶς (pä's) – all, all things, everything, all men, whole

Matthew 3:10, 4:4, 5:15,18, Ephesians 3:19–21

Thank you:

Know:

Grow:

Go:

Flow:

Sow:

Get Low:

Living Stone 1 PETER 2:5

Moment 22 – Luke 22
Savor & Reflect: Acts 9:31
   God: Jehovah Tsidkenu (The Lord Our Righteousness)
   Jeremiah 23:6, 33:16
Ruminating Prayer: Grant me peace today as I live in fear of You and not of mankind.

Judas was a man chosen to live with God, seeing miracles daily and living in a personal relationship with Jesus. Judas was tempted and chose to trade eternal life for an ephemeral treasure. Where our treasure resides can be seen through our dreams, words, and actions. We must be on guard and in relationship with people who fight the lies Satan wants us to believe, a lie that our earthly wants and needs are more important than God's Kingdom.

The physical world where we live is merely the prequel to the Kingdom of God. The time we value today is the basis for our relationship with God for eternity. It sets the stage for our purpose in the presence of God. Invest in your tomorrows by being Kingdom focused today.

Peter failed with Christ over and over again. He failed the Son of God at the cross, and yet Jesus forgave him and used him for God's glory. Jesus loved both Peter and Judas by washing their feet and eating with them at Passover. Jesus loves you! Your past, present, or future sins will never define you in Christ. You are covered in the love of Christ, His soul-redeeming blood makes you free to draw close to God in prayer, and identify with Him as your foundation while living daily.

Greek: οἰκοδομέω (oikodomeō) – to build up, to rebuild, to promote growth in Christian wisdom, grace, holiness

Matthew 7:26, 16:18, Luke 4:29, John 2:20, Acts 7:47,49

Thank you:

Know:

Grow:

Go:

Flow:

Sow:

Get Low:

Vessel of
Mercy & Honor ROMANS 9:21-24

Moment 23 – Luke 23
Savor & Reflect: 2 Timothy 2:21
 God: Jehovah Rapha/Rophe (The Lord Who Heals)
 Genesis 20:17, 50:2
Ruminating Prayer: Master, Speak and I will do Your good work.

In Luke 10, Jesus shares the parable of the Good Samaritan to help Christ followers understand that being kind is an expectation we have but often do not show. Our kindness is not just for people like us but for those we put in the box labeled "other" that should be labeled "brother."

Two sinners were treated as equals with Jesus when they were crucified with Him. A killer was freed so Jesus could give His life for us and now we are free, to live a new life as we trust Him daily. Jesus loves the sinner! He cannot stand sin, and in love He came, lived among us, and died for you and every person in the world who bears His image.

The temple of God was where God's presence was seen and known by God's people. Priests, chosen interceders, would enter the temple on behalf of others and themselves to take gifts (sacrificial offerings) to God as part of their apology for sin. The temple had two halves separated by a curtain to keep people away from judgment, God's Holiness. When Jesus died, the temple curtain was torn in two, the Holy of Holies was exposed so broken people could go before and to God through Jesus. Where God is, is where He can be heard and known. Where God is moving is where you want to be. Jesus is our High Priest, and God's Spirit lives in you. You are the temple of God.

Greek: ἁγιάζω (hagiazō) – sanctify, hallow, to be holy

Matthew 23:17–19, Luke 11:2, Acts 20:32, 26:18

Thank you:

Know:

Grow:

Go:

Flow:

Sow:

Get Low:

Made MATTHEW 22:37-40

Moment 24 – Luke 24
Savor & Reflect: Numbers 23:19
    God: Jehovah Rapha/Rophe (The Lord Who Heals)
    Exodus 15:26, 21:19
Ruminating Prayer: Make my mind like Your word, refreshing, and unchanging.

What is your favorite sport to watch? What is your favorite sport to play? The difference between playing a sport and watching a sport is substantial. You are expected to be more than a fan, and you are not just playing a game called life. You have been chosen to be a follower of Christ and to do the hard work of being an agent of change, that is, the salt and light that highlight the truth of Jesus in every situation and relationship. You are made to serve God and others in ways that matter for eternity.

Every day we take actions that can be centered in love if we are willing to put God first. Daily we must renew our minds with the words of God the same way athletes exercise. We live like we train, and we live for tomorrow.

Jesus ate, shared, and journeyed with His disciples to show them He was—and is—alive. He encouraged His disciples to not stand in awe of awesomeness but to be a witness to others of God's power. We are to share the truth of His resurrection, the opportunity of redemption in Him, and how Jesus fulfilled the promises of the prophets. Our minds must stay centered in Christ because this is not a game, but an opportunity to work with God.

Greek: διάνοια (de-ä'-noi-ä) – source of understanding, feelings, desires, and thoughts.

Mark 12:30, Luke 1:51, 10:27, Ephesians 1:8, 2:3, Colossians 1:21

Thank you:

Know:

Grow:

Go:

Flow:

Sow:

Get Low:

Sheeple JOHN 10:1-16

Moment 25 – Acts 1
Savor & Reflect: John 10:27–28
    God: Jehovah Rapha/Rophe (The Lord Who Heals)
    Job 5:18, 13:4
Ruminating Prayer: You call me Your own, You know me, and nothing can separate us.

Jesus calls His followers sheep, and His sheep know His voice. Knowing the voice of Jesus comes from spending an extravagant amount of time with Him. He causes us to know Him as our hearts experience highs and lows with Him.

A unique aspect of sheep in comparison to giraffes is that sheep have a limited view of the world around them because of how they were created. The disciples, before Jesus ascended to Heaven, assumed He was going to change the world in a way that they wanted. Jesus made it clear that our role is not to lead but to follow Jesus and He will give us the information we need moment by moment.

The Holy Spirit was given to us to train us in truth and love. You have God, the Holy Spirit, within you. The Spirit of God is living within you; He is interceding with the rest of God on your behalf. Knowing and working with the Holy Spirit require us to listen well, engage, and obey Him. To obey with greater insight and understanding, we must be filled with God's Words. Make time to read God's word while listening and talking to His Spirit throughout the day. How are we, followers of our Good Shepherd, like sheep?

Greek: μάρτυς (mä'r-tüs) – a witness, martyr, record

Luke 24:48, Philippians 1:8, Hebrews 12:1, Revelation 1:5

Thank you:

Know:

Grow:

Go:

Flow:

Sow:

Get Low:

Light EPHESIANS 5:1-8

Moment 26 – Acts 2
Savor & Reflect: John 10:27–28
    God: El Elyon (The Most High God)
    Genesis 14:18–22
Ruminating Prayer: With just a word, Father, You separated the light from the darkness.

As a child of the Light, as a child of God, being a reflection of God, choose today to be a living sacrifice to God; sacrifice your thoughts, words, and actions. God has made you family with Him, which means you are called to live better than you did yesterday and to respond differently toward the world around you. Your thoughts, words, and actions must be renewed daily as you identify with Him.

Where does your time go in the day? What do you do to relax? Often the things we identify with the most in the day get the most of our day. Our work, playtime, and time for prayer often allow us to see our heart's focus.

Our identification with our Heavenly Father creates the space to yield to His voice as we engage and are transformed within Him and grow with those He created to be family. When you and others come together to worship God, you are the Church, but the Church is not a building. Worshiping God is what believers are created for, and when we do it around others, we are a light in the world. When you love those who don't love you, you attract people to Christ. What drew you to the Light? Let others see and feel the Light in you.

Hebrew:אור (ore) – light, the light of day, daybreak, bright

Genesis 1:4–5, Zephaniah 3:5, Zechariah 14:6–7

Thank you:

Know:

Grow:

Go:

Flow:

Sow:

Get Low:

Salt MATTHEW 5:13-16

Moment 27 – Acts 3
Savor & Reflect: Acts 3:9
    God: El Elyon (The Most High God)
    Numbers 24:16, Deuteronomy 26:19, 28:1
Ruminating Prayer: I don't care who sees, I will praise You and walk with You today.

We have an incredible opportunity today to effect change in the world around us by living out our faith. Our faith is dynamic, because it is centered in Jesus and just like our Savior, we must do more than talk for people to feel the love of God. Your faith isn't solely for you. Your faith is meant to make the community around you better because you put others first. Salty followers share life sacrificially because of Christ's sacrifice.

What you listen to, others will hear in you as it comes out of your heart. What you watch on your devices, others will see in you. Be mindful that your heart now belongs to God, and the fruit of His Spirit is the salt you share with others.

The work of being salt in the world is hard work, because the world does not understand your motivation, Jesus' sacrifice. Therefore, all they see is your personal sacrifice without the love that drives it. When you keep the truth of grace and mercy that took place on Calvary in your mind, then it makes your daily sacrifice a joy. Today, you have an opportunity to be a blessing by distinctly living out your faith through humbly loving others. Strive to make every encounter today better than you found it.

Greek: πεντηκοστή (pentēkostē) – filled to overflowing, the seventh week after the Passover, Pentecost

Exodus 23:26, Leviticus 23:15, Acts 2:1, 20:16,

Thank you:

Know:

Grow:

Go:

Flow:

Sow:

Get Low:

New Body, New Home LUKE 20:34-36

Moment 28 – Acts 4
Savor & Reflect: Acts 4:31
    God: El Elyon (The Most High God)
    Psalm 50:14, 57:2, 78:35
Ruminating Prayer: I am filled with Your Holy Spirit;
I will speak Your Word courageously today, my God.

Being courageous is speaking when others are quiet and listening when others are loud. Courageousness comes in having a rational fear of God and what He can do, and an acceptance that He is free to exercise His power as He sees fit. It takes courage to tell the truth encircled in love.

Peter and John, disciples of Christ— like you—were ordered to stop sharing the truth they saw, experienced, and were living in Christ. Their lives were threatened because the leaders of the day could not understand what they were saying. The leaders allowed fear and pride to rule in their hearts instead of being humbled or seeking to learn and follow Jesus. We must make a choice to follow the leading of the Holy Spirit by fearing God more than men.

The same Spirit you are reading about today is the same Living Spirit who lives in you. The power you are reading about is not found in the people but in their willingness to be used by God. When you pray, pray with God's will in mind, with a focus on seeing people changed. By having real relationships through His Son, the Christ, you are conversing with God about the things that bring Him joy. Jesus is the Way, the Truth, and the Life. No person can know God without a personal humbling repentant relationship with Jesus. To be fully used by Him, resolve to reconcile being a living sacrifice, daily, filled with His Spirit.

Greek: εἷς (heis) – one, one man, unity within the whole

Matthew 5:18–19, Matthew 18:10,12,14, 16, Acts 4:32

Thank you:

Know:

Grow:

Go:

Flow:

Sow:

Get Low:

Blessed MATTHEW 5:3-4

Moment 29 – Acts 5
Savor & Reflect: Acts 5:29
  God: Jehovah Mekoddishkem (Lord Who Sanctifies
  You)
  Genesis 2:3, Exodus 13:2, 19:10
Ruminating Prayer: Heavenly Father, Jesus, and the
Holy Spirit, I will obey You instead of people.

As children we learn to obey. For some, obeying comes
easy because children know love through their parents.
For others, obedience is hard because they believe no
one cares for them. Our hearts respond differently to
yielding to God based on how we view Him.

Why would God allow His disciples to be taken away?
They were healing the sick; the Spirit of God was
moving. They were living out the truth of love! Everyone
in every place needs to hear the truth of what Jesus has
done, and the risk is always worth it as long as we yield
our daily interactions to glorify God. People need to
experience forgiveness and abundant life. When we ask
the why about situations, we often miss the Who. Who is
in charge? God is, and we are to worship Him wherever
He leads us.

Ananias and Sapphira lied to God by giving a gift to impress others before God. They did not fear the Living God fully; their lack of respect and understanding caused them to be an example of scorn. Our motives— our heart behind our actions—matter more than the gifts we bring, because God does not need anything. Be a blessing to those God brings across your path today. Bring your motives and moments before your Master, Lord. He will turn these moments into milestones with intentional obedience.

Greek: ψεύδομαι (pseudomai) – to lie, to speak to deceive, to speak falsehoods

Matthew 5:11, Acts 5:3-4, Romans 9:1

Thank you:

Know:

Grow:

Go:

Flow:

Sow:

Get Low:

Blessed MATTHEW 5:5-6

Moment 30 – Acts 6
Savor & Reflect: Acts 6:5
> God: Jehovah Mekoddishkem (Lord Who Sanctifies You)
> Exodus 20:8, 11, 30:29–30

Ruminating Prayer: Holy Spirit, Spirit of the Living God, make my faith full in You.

Your faith is given to you by God and is centered in the loving actions of Jesus on the cross. It will be completed when you stand before the Messiah in His throne room, heaven. YOU—and all people—have a purpose that is greater than yourself. Your purpose in Christ is best understood within dynamic communities. Your spiritual gifts should be used to serve others in a way that allows them to experience God's love. Be a blessing!

Being a blessing does not mean your life will be easy. You may have to die physically so others can know God. Being a blessing means being meek, hungering, and thirsting for righteousness. It means being like Christ. Being a blessing means being with God and working where He is working.

God works through us when we listen and look for ways to obey Him. Listening to God means creating space in our schedule to do the things that challenge us like fellowshipping and caring for homeless people, incarcerated people, and other broken people like us.

Hebrew: χάρις (khä'-res) – grace, goodwill, a gift of grace, thanks

Luke 1:30, 2:40, John 1:14, 16–17, Acts 6:8

Thank you:

Know:

Grow:

Go:

Flow:

Sow:

Get Low:

Reflection WHAT DOES SALVATION MEAN TO YOU? WHO IS JESUS TO YOU?

Moment 31 – Let Christ be your standard, ask for help with weakness, and celebrate His work in your life.

What have you learned through the last seven days in your relationship with God?

What will you do today that is different because of what you learned?

What step will you do to make this a habit?

What was your favorite Bible verse(s) from the last few days and why?

What was your favorite name for God so far and why?

31 People you are asking God to make new in Him.
Name, date you started praying, their story, old and new birthdates

1. _____

2. _____

3. _____

4. _____

5. _____

6. _____

7. _____

8. _____

9. _____

10. _____

11. _____

12. _____

13. _____

14. _____

15. _____

16. _____

17. _____

18. _____

19. _____

20. _____

21. _____

22. _____

23. _____

24. _____

25. _____

26. _____

27. _____

28. _____

29. _____

30. _____

31. _____

Ideas, Dreams and Visions